Electronic Projects for Model Aircraft

To David and Claire

Electronic Projects for Model Aircraft

Ken Ginn

Nexus Special Interests

Nexus Special Interests Ltd.
Nexus House
Azalea Drive
Swanley
Kent BR8 8HU

First published in Great Britain by Nexus Special Interests Ltd., 1998

ISBN 1-85486-178-6

Typeset by Kate Williams, Abergavenny
Printed and bound in Great Britain by Biddles Ltd., Guildford & King's Lynn

Contents

Acknowledgements

I would like to thank Clive Rainbird for his assistance with the project ideas in the making of this book

■ 1
Introduction

Outlined within the pages of this book are a number of projects that can be attempted by the modeller to assist in the running and maintenance of electronic systems associated with model aircraft, some of which can also apply to other radio control models such as cars and boats.

Although the majority of the projects are designed to be constructed with relative ease, a few projects, however, require construction techniques and a keen eye. The use of surface mount devices (SMDs) in a specific instance has been incorporated to reduce the amount of space on the printed circuit board (PCB) in some cases, but elsewhere the use of standard components have been used where component space is considered not to be a priority.

It is up to the modeller to source components from a local supplier, or by mail order and checking the availability of specific components is advised before attempting to construct the projects. No specialist components are needed or need to be programmed. The only possible problem obtaining a small percentage of the components would be the SMDs. A UK supplier for these SMD integrated circuits is given in Appendix A. Indeed, should you wish to redesign the PCB to suit your need, the SMD integrated circuits can be bought in dual-in-line (DIL) form – the pin assignments are the same shown in the circuit diagrams for both forms.

Tools

The tools needed to construct the projects are very basic and are available from electronic component suppliers. However, additional tools will be required should certain projects be attempted.

Apart from the tools required to fabricate the case for each project, a number of additional tools for the electronics are needed. They are:

- Needle-nose pliers
- Small wire cutters
- Large wire cutters
- Soldering iron (³⁄₁₆ inch bit)
- Desoldering braid (may be useful)
- Desolder pump
- Screwdrivers (assorted)
- Electric high speed PCB drill
- Assorted drills

Additional tools required for soldering surface mount components on the board are as follows:

- Soldering iron with surface mount bit
- Surface mount solder paste.

A number of high speed steel (HSS) twist drill bits are needed to drill and enlarge holes on the PCB should the supply of components vary and lead sizes be different than those encountered in the prototypes. Common sizes of twist drill are 0.6mm, 0.8mm, 1.0mm and 1.2mm. Additional drills may be needed to mount a PCB relay or perhaps a PCB mounting heatsink used in a couple of the projects. The use of HSS drills is preferred, despite these types of drill having a shorter life than the tungsten carbide variety. The latter are less tolerant to use with hand-held drills, however, the use of a purpose-made high speed pillar drill works better with tungsten carbide drills. Tungsten carbide twist drills require a certain amount of care when in use.

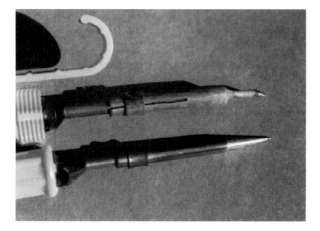

Soldering irons.
Top – ³⁄₁₆ bit, bottom – SMD bit.

Printed circuit boards

Production techniques of PCBs are not covered in this book. Details of PCB layouts are given in each chapter, and in some cases a PCB layout is also detailed, shown enlarged to twice its size due to the small size of the actual completed circuit board.

Appendix A lists a company willing to produce the PCBs as one-offs or in quantity. However, I hope this will not stop you from producing the boards yourself – there are a number that can be using various methods.

Surface mount components

In a commercial world SMDs are mounted onto a PCB in an automated assembly. These components are stuck with a spot of glue onto the board by machine and then soldered to the board. Without the expense of automated machinery and producing one-offs for personal requirements, the builder requires some ingenuity in producing jigs to assist in the mounting of components to the PCB.

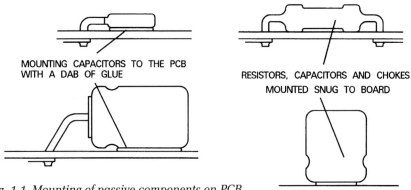

MOUNTING CAPACITORS TO THE PCB
WITH A DAB OF GLUE

RESISTORS, CAPACITORS AND CHOKES
MOUNTED SNUG TO BOARD

Fig. 1.1 Mounting of passive components on PCB.

The size of the surface mount integrated circuit is minute in comparison to its DIL cousin. The pin spacing, for example, between the adjacent pins is actually half that of the DIL integrated circuits, the row spacing being less also. In fact, the surface mount integrated circuit is getting closer in size to the actual semiconductor chip within the surface mount package therefore more care has to be exercised with SMDs when handling and also when soldering these devices onto the board.

Static sensitive devices

A large proportion of integrated circuits produced today, and indeed discrete semiconductor devices such as transistors and some diodes, are termed as static sensitive devices (SSDs). Essentially this means that if these devices are mishandled in such a way as to build up a static charge in the device, immediate or premature failure could result. Therefore it is wise to consider a few precautions when handling these components to ensure no damage is done.

Do not handle SSD devices prior to actually installing them into the circuit proper, i.e. plugging them into IC sockets or soldering them into the board. Keep them in the supplier's original anti-static packaging until the component is needed to be soldered in or placed circuit, such as with the use of IC sockets. This will reduce the chance of static build-up on the device.

Arrange a SSD handling area, away from nylon carpets and any likely source of static. Use a SSD wrist strap; this will slowly discharge any charge which may have built up on the body. The wrist strap is actually connected to earth via a 1 MΩ resistor – mains earth is sufficient. This will allow any static charge to safely flow away. SSD earthing kits are available from suppliers.

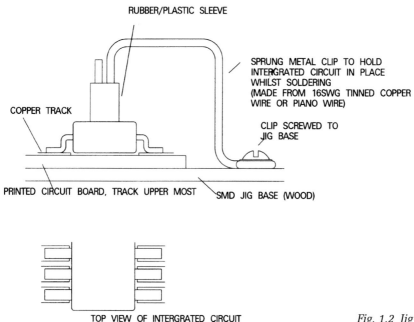

Fig. 1.2 Jig for holding SMD devices while soldering.

The mounting of SSD devices, and this includes SMD devices, can be carried out initially, such as the first components to populate a board. Should this approach be adopted, then the whole PCB has to be treated as one SSD device. It may be easier where SMD devices are used to first solder the SMD devices to the PCB, then to add the remaining components afterwards. Treat the board as though it were a complete SSD device and use an earthed wrist strap until the board is completed, and even then treat the board with care. By far the best approach is to complete the board with all the passive components, then add the SSD at the last part of the construction.

Mounting surface mount components

Mounting surface mount components needs some skill and a good eye. First, the board has to be securely fastened to a rigid or solid work surface. With a small length of tinned copper wire place a small dab of solder paste on all the PCB pads where the component is to be placed. Do not be tempted to put too much paste on the pad as there is the likelihood that a short will occur between the pad you wish to solder and an adjacent pad. It can be difficult then to remove this short circuit – using the desolder braid will be handy here.

Once the paste has been applied to the component's pad, orientate the component ensuring that the pins are in correct alignment. The component leads should be placed squarely on the pads on the board and in the middle of each pad.

Using a fine-tipped soldering iron, tinned, apply heat to the joint and watch as the solder paste completes the joint. Each joint takes only a second or so to complete. It is recommended that a 15 W soldering iron be used for this particular job. These minute components will heat up very rapidly indeed due to the low thermal mass of the component, so the action of soldering in the component must be completed swiftly otherwise internal damage could occur.

Once surface mount components or, for that matter, any components have been soldered on to the PCB, a visual inspection of the track side of the board is a must. This inspection will ensure that any solder bridges or dry joints are spotted and rectified before the board is put into use. Otherwise an expensive mistake may be made, and components may then have to replaced.

Test equipment

Most modellers will not be equipped with sophisticated electronic test equipment, such as an oscilloscope, signal sources or power supplies, which although expensive would actually assist greatly the setting up of a number of the projects. The use of this type of equipment should be discouraged purely on cost grounds, but it is recommended that a digital multimeter (DMM) be obtained to assist in the setting up and construction of these projects.

A DMM may also prove itself an invaluable tool in fault finding, the setting up of future projects and also problems encountered in the field. Given time it will become an essential part of a tool box.

DMMs can be purchased from a number of outlets, with a number of facilities incorporated. Basically the instrument should be capable of measuring resistance (to 20 MΩ), voltage AC and DC (600V), and current (DC) with a maximum current reading range of 10 amps (A). With this specification, one such DMM should be available at a reasonable cost. Of course, should there be additional features incorporated, the cost will rise accordingly.

Lastly where used in a specific project, test components are specified within the component listing to assist the setting up of each project. These components are specific to each project and obviate the need for some types of additional test equipment.

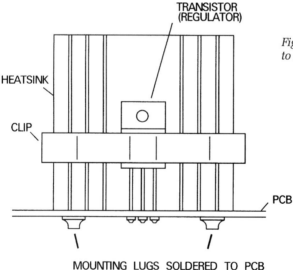

Fig. 1.3 Mounting power semiconductors to PCB heatsinks.

Component mounting

Where possible, it is preferable to mount the components close to the actual surface of the PCB. This will assist greatly in the reliability of the specific component where otherwise considerable stress and vibration to the component is possible, such as in airborne systems. Large components, such as electrolytic capacitors, can be placed horizontally down and stuck to the PCB. This will have the effect of reducing the stress between the soldered lead of the component and the body of the component.

In the prototypes, sockets have been utilised in order to mount the DIL components. If the project being built is to be utilised in an airborne environment it is best that any DIL component (an integrated circuit) be soldered straight into the PCB.

Protection

In a model a number of means can be provided to protect the completed project installed, one being a purpose-built box, fabricated from balsa which will offer some degree of protection to the circuits. Balsa has the great advantage that is light in weight. Alternatively the circuit can be enclosed in a small plastic enclosure, but this may prove impracticable, due to weight constraints. Should the completed circuit be laid bare in the model, it would be wise to cover the circuit with some form of protection. A spray rather like a clear lacquer, known as a conformal coating, should be applied in several layers to the component and trackside of the circuit after completion and setting up. This will provide a good degree of protection to the circuit against moisture penetration.

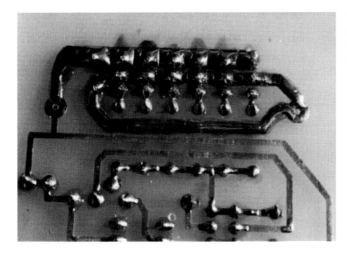

This photo illustrates the technique of building up tracks with solder to reduce track resistance on high current carrying paths.

Cabling

In each project various types of cable are used – be certain the gauge of wire used in each case is adequate for the job. Where motor currents are particularly high, the cabling has to be capable of carrying that current otherwise the result could be cable heating, meaning a loss of power to the model's motor. In projects where high currents are anticipated, the same problem occurs on the PCB tracks. Here the track can be built up on the PCB with a soldering iron and solder in order to increase the solder thickness and thus reduce the track resistance.

■ 2

Tx/Rx Battery Charger

The battery charger described here is designed to charge a number of nicad batteries from the one mains powered charger. The use of the charger is designed such that prior to a day's flying, the transmitter's and receiver's nicad batteries can all be charged overnight. This could include a total of two transmitters and three receiver batteries.

Completed charger PCB.

Five independent charging outputs are provided which can have a choice of two charging currents and are independently selected with the aid of a push button switch. Any output can be used to charge receiver or transmitter batteries. The charging current is independent of whether a receiver or transmitter battery pack is being charged as long as the charged battery voltage does not exceed 17 V.

9

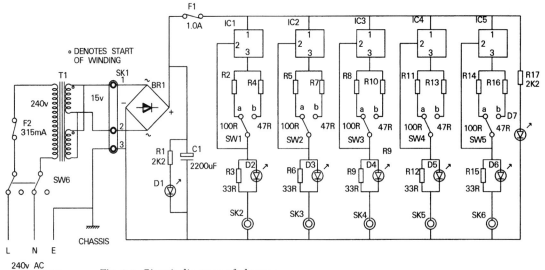

Fig. 2.1 Circuit diagram of charger.

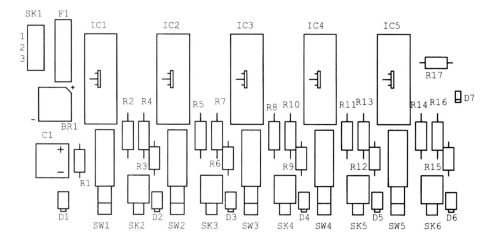

Fig. 2.2

The circuit

The mains voltage is transformed down to 15 V AC with the mains transformer T1. The bridge rectifier BR1 converts the alternating current to a direct current, and being further smoothed by C1 produces a DC voltage of 25 V off load which will drop under load, i.e. when the unit is used to charge batteries.

The unit uses five identical circuits to provide constant current to charge a maximum of five battery packs, each being independent of the neighbouring circuit.

Each charging circuit is a simple circuit which uses a 5 V, 1 A voltage regulator to provide a stable charging constant current. The action of the regulator is to provide across the load resistor (example R2) a stable voltage; this will be 5 V. The current which will flow through this load resistor will depend largely on the load resistor's value. The charging current can be gained from Ohm's Law, thus:

$$\text{Charging current I (A)}= \frac{5.0}{\text{Load (R)}}$$

For example, the charging current of 50 mA (45 mA) would require a resistance value of 100 ohm (Ω), 100 mA – 47 Ω.

Visual indication is also provided with the charger to show that charging current is being supplied to the battery pack with an LED. The LED itself has a maximum current value at which it is rated (30 mA), and this is below the minimum charging current mentioned so far (50 mA). A resistor (a value of 33 Ω) is selected to shunt the current away from the LED, such that sufficient current safely goes through the LED to illuminate it when charging a battery. The majority of the charging current is shunted around to this additional resistor, thus keeping the LED running within its maximum current rating. The value of the resistor chosen here is safe for currents up to 120 mA. It will be noted that when the charger is in use, the brightness of the LED will change as a different value of charging current is chosen; this is normal.

Two additional LEDs are mounted on the PCB. One is viewed from the outside and indicates the mains supply is supplied and the unit is switched on. A second LED (D7) is mounted inside the unit and is present to facilitate fault finding, if, for any reason, the fuse on the PCB blows (F1). In the event of a fault occurring with the unit, the power LED (D1) may still be illuminated, and D7 is unlit. It would be safe to assume in this situation the low voltage fuse on the PCB (F1) has blown.

Replacement of any fuse on the unit is best carried out with the unit switched off and disconnected from a mains power source, for safety reasons.

Construction

The majority of the components are constructed on a single sided PCB, with the exception of the mains transformer (T1), mains power switch (SW6) and mains fuse F2. These components are mounted on the enclosure. The access to the charging sockets, charging current LEDs and charging current selector switches are provided from the front of the PCB.

In the prototype, charging currents of 50 mA and 100 mA were chosen to enable nicad packs of 480 mAH and 1000 mAH to be charged for the recommended 14 hour charging period. However, it is possible to charge a 1600 mAH set of nicads, at a charging current of 160mA, by changing the load resistor value accordingly to 33 Ω. The resistor used to bypass the charging current through the appropriate charging LED would have to be reduced to 18 Ω, to avoid overloading the LED.

The PCB is mounted to the base of the enclosure and is spaced away from the bottom of the enclosure with the aid of PCB spacers. The mains transformer T1 is mounted to the rear of the enclosure as shown. It would be wise to use lengths of plastic sleeving (about 15 mm) where mains voltages are present, for example, on the terminals of the fuse holder F2, mains switch SW7 and the transformer primary winding T1. This will increase the safety of the unit when the cover is off, during testing. Lengths of plastic sleeving are also advisable on the transformer low voltage secondary terminals.

Checking out the unit

Once the unit has been constructed a visual inspection of the PCB is needed to ensure that there are no mistakes, solder bridges or dry joints. Check the wiring also.

As this unit is powered from a mains power supply certain safety precautions have to be considered.

The following checks should be made with the unit disconnected from a mains supply. First, check the resistance with the aid of a multimeter between the mains plug 'earth' pin to the metal chassis of the charger – this should be as low as possible, certainly less than 1.0 Ω. With the mains power switch in the 'on' position, check the resistance between the mains plug 'earth' pin and the 'live' pin of the mains plug, then the resistance between the 'earth' and the 'neutral' pin of the mains plug. Both these readings should be high, certainly higher than 20 MΩ. The resistance between the 'live' and 'neutral' pins on the mains plug should read below 20 Ω, i.e. low, reading the primary resistance of the mains transformer (T1). Using the charger's power switch, turn the switch to the off position – the resistance reading from 'live' to 'neutral' should rise to above 20 MΩ.

Check the resistance from the earth pin of the mains plug to the negative (0 V) side of the charger – this should be low, less than 1.0 Ω.

Lastly, now check the insulation resistance from the primary to the secondary of the mains transformer – this should be shown to be greater than 20 MΩ.

Connect the unit to the mains supply and switch the charger on. Set the multimeter to a DC voltage range and set to read at least 30 V. Connect the multimeter probes across the positive terminal and the negative terminal if the bridge rectifier BR1. The voltage on the multimeter should read in the region of 25 V, DC.

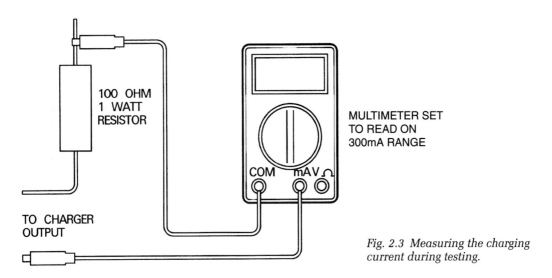

100 OHM
1 WATT
RESISTOR

MULTIMETER SET
TO READ ON
300mA RANGE

COM   mAV Ω

TO CHARGER
OUTPUT

Fig. 2.3 Measuring the charging current during testing.

Connect a load resistor of 100 Ω across each charger output with the multimeter in series, and set to read DC current, as shown in Figure 2.3. The test 100 Ω resister will simulate a battery pack. Select a charging current as required on the current switch; the multimeter will then read the charging current, for example 50 mA. The LED for that particular charging circuit will then illuminate. Choosing the other charging current higher or lower in value, will either make the LED glow brighter or dimmer. Check this second charging current. The charging current on each range should fall within the following limits: 40 to 50 mA for the 50 mA setting, and 90 to 110 mA for the 100 mA setting.

Connecting the Tx and Rx to the charger

To connect any battery to the charger will require a purpose-made lead to be manufactured. First, the charging connector at the battery side (including transmitters) has to be ascertained. Secondly the polarity of this plug has also to be confirmed. Label each charging lead as different manufacturers may have similar charging plugs, but with different connections.

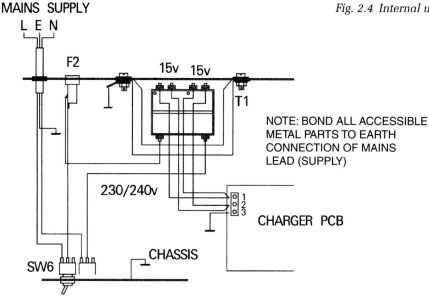

MAINS SUPPLY

Fig. 2.4 Internal unit wiring.

NOTE: BOND ALL ACCESSIBLE
METAL PARTS TO EARTH
CONNECTION OF MAINS
LEAD (SUPPLY)

CHARGER PCB

With the original mains powered charger connected to the mains power supply, connect a multimeter across the original charger's output connector and observe the polarity of the voltage at this point. Make a note of this – this is very important.

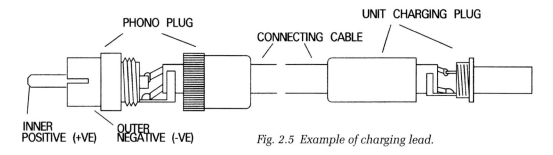

Fig. 2.5 Example of charging lead.

Make the new lead up, connecting the new charging connector to one end of the lead, and a phono connector to the other end of the lead. Note that the outer conductor of the phono socket and plug is negative, and the inner conductor positive.

Check the new lead for breaks in the lead, from end to end and shorts between the wires within the new lead with the aid of a multimeter. A shorted charging lead could cause the charging battery to be shorted out when the charger is in use and the battery could suffer permanent damage as a result. The charger should not suffer any damage should this type of fault occur.

14

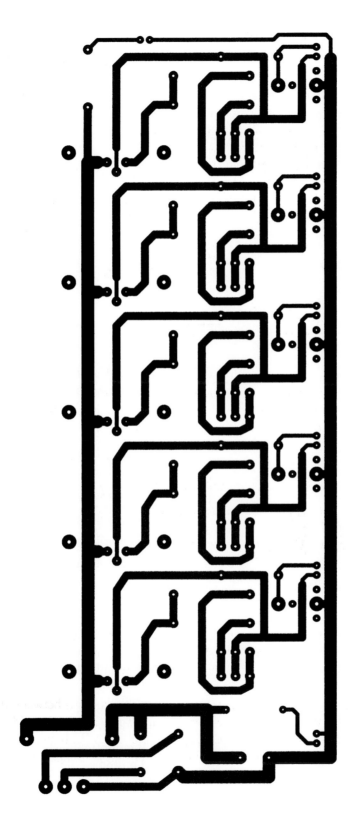

Fig. 2.6 PCB shown through from component side (actual size).

Conclusion

The charger can be used to replace a multitude of individual chargers connected to a large number of models. The one charger can now quite simply charge five sets of batteries at one time.

The time taken to charge a set of discharged batteries with this unit is set to fourteen hours. It is designed to follow the battery manufacturer's charging times, thus ensuring the battery, if in a good condition, will store as much of the charge given to it throughout the charging cycle.

Component list

R1	2K2 ½ W		IC3	7805 5 V 1 A regulator
R2	100R 2 W		IC4	7805 5 V 1 A regulator
R3	33R ½ W		IC5	7805 5 V 1 A regulator
R4	47R 1 W		BR1	400 V 2 A bridge rectifier, Maplin stock no: AQ99H
R5	100R 1 W		D1	PCB mounting LED green, Maplin stock no: QY87U
R6	33R ½ W			
R7	47R 1 W		D2	PCB mounting LED red, Maplin stock no: QY86T
R8	100R 1 W			
R9	33R ½ W		D3	PCB mounting LED red
R10	47R 1 W		D4	PCB mounting LED red
R11	100R 1 W		D5	PCB mounting LED red
R12	33R ½ W		D6	PCB mounting LED red
R13	47R 1 W		D7	LED, red
R14	100R 1 W		SW1	PCB mounting push button switch, and button, Maplin stock no: FH67X
R15	33R ½ W			
R16	47R 1 W			
R17	2K2 ½ W		SW2	PCB mounting push button switch, and button
C1	2200µF 35V PCB mounting electrolytic			
			SW3	PCB mounting push button switch, and button
IC1	7805 5 V 1 A regulator, Maplin stock no: CH35Q			
			SW4	PCB mounting push button switch, and button
IC2	7805 5 V 1 A regulator			

SW5   PCB mounting push button switch, and button

SW6   DPDT toggle switch, rated at mains voltages 240 V AC

F1   PCB mounting fuse holder and fuse (1.0 amp), Maplin stock no: KU29G

T1   Mains transformer 240 V primary, 15 V 1.6 A (2 × 15 V 830 mA secondaries connected in parallel) secondary (25 VA), Maplin stock no: DH27E

Miscellaneous components

■ Heatsinks for regulators (5) Maplin stock no: AX95D
■ Clips for regulators (5) Maplin stock no: AX97F
■ Terminal (SK1)
■ Case
■ Wire
■ Charger plugs
■ Chassis mounting fuse holder and fuse, and leads.

■ 3
Fast Nicad Charger

In electric-powered model aircraft the source of motive power for the motor is usually a nickel cadmium rechargeable battery (nicad). The particular type of nicad used in these applications is the sintered cell type of battery which can deliver the higher currents drawn by the motor during flight.

One problem with nicads is quite often the battery is exhausted after a flight of only five or ten minutes. This is due to the limited amount of energy stored in a battery. To get any

Fast nicad charger.

reasonable overall flying time with a model during a day, the battery has to be charged a number of times. The normal charging time for nicad batteries is fourteen hours, but for a sintered cell nicad the charging time can be much reduced. The need then is to recharge the sintered cell nicad at a much higher current in order to reduce the battery charging time. One trade off with the higher charging current and shorter charging time is apparent; the battery is less efficient at taking up the charge at a high charge current than utilising a charger in a slower charging cycle. That is, the lower the charging current the greater the efficiency of the battery taking the overall charge.

When charging at this higher rate, for example at twice the amp hour capacity of the battery, certain care has to be exercised. There is a risk of the battery exploding if the current is too high, despite there being a safety valve built into each battery cell. The charging time of the battery also has to be adhered to. Failure to do this can result in the cells producing too much gas and failing prematurely.

In this chapter certain criteria has been set out. First, a constant current charger circuit is used to charge the battery. Secondly, a clockwork timer is utilised to set the timing period and thirdly, the technique of pulse charging the battery is utilised (this is briefly explained).

One other point relevant to the charging of nicads, and is used here is the technique of pulse charging the battery. This helps the cells take up more of the charging current than would otherwise be achieved with a constant direct current charger. In this application this technique has been chosen.

Use of the charger

The charger is capable of charging either a six, seven or eight cell pack from a 12 volt (V) DC source. The intended power source in the field is a 12 V car battery. The charger is set to one of two battery capacities, for example 1200 mAH or 1400 mAH capacities, the appropriate capacity, and hence charging current is selected with the aid of SW2. The charger is set to charge the battery pack for a period of up to 30 minutes. Once it has completed the pulse fast charge cycle of the battery the battery will then trickle charge at approximately 75 mA, and will remain trickle charging until the battery is removed from the charger unit.

Circuit diagram

The unit can be split into three main parts. The first section is the mechanical timer – this selects the charging time. When the charging cycle is started, by rotating the timer control,

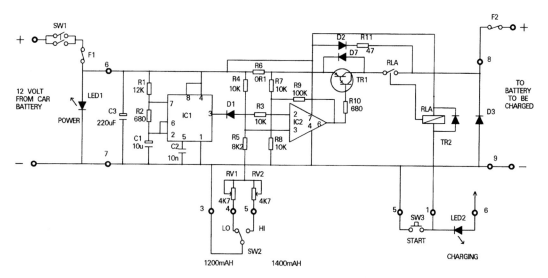

Fig. 3.1 Fast nicad charger circuit diagram.

the clockwork timer switch SW3 contacts close energising the relay RLA and providing pulse charging current to the battery. The relay RLA will remain energised during the charging cycle, the period of which is selected by the timer.

The second part of the unit is the constant current charger circuit, which is designed as a source to run from a 12 V supply, i.e. a 12 V car battery for field work. Also, to charge nicads to a charged terminal voltage of 10.5 V, the drop out voltage (the difference between the input and the output voltage) has to be as low as possible for the charger to operate successfully. This circuit uses a resistor (R6) to sense the current drawn through the charger, the error voltage is sensed at each side of R6 and is fed to the error amplifier IC2. The output from IC1 is fed to TR1 which adjusts the charging voltage at the battery terminal in such a way as to maintain a constant current charging the battery. This current is kept within some five per cent of the set charging current throughout the whole charging cycle of the battery. This technique is more successful than a simple series current limiting resistor between the 12 V source and the charging battery.

The final part of the unit is the pulse generator IC1, an NE555; this supplies pulses to the error amplifier in order to switch it on and off during the charging cycle. These pulses are applied to the error amplifier and switch the amplifier on and off. The pulse generator produces pulses at a rate of approximately 10 Hz. The high (on) duration of the pulse is 92 ms, and the low (off) duration is 5 ms, thus producing an overall high accumulated charging current with very little off charging time. The loss of charging current during this 'off' is not a drawback, as the system of pulse charging a battery is more efficient.

Construction

The circuit is constructed on a single sided PCB, and mounted within a metal enclosure. Most of the components are mounted on this board, with the exception of the power switch SW1, SW2, the timer unit incorporating SW3, the two LED indicators and the two fuses and their holders. Should a problem occur when charging a battery in the field it is best to replace a fuse accessible on the outside of the unit rather than replace it on the PCB, thereby having to open the unit.

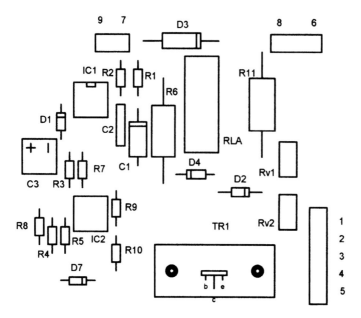

Fig. 3.2 Component layout.

Mount R6 and R11 with a little air between the body of the resistor and the PCB to allow ventilation as these components may become a little warm during use. Otherwise all the rest of the components can be mounted snug to the board.

Mount the two ICs in sockets.

The internal wiring of the unit is accomplished as shown in Figure 3.3. Some of the internal wiring has to carry high currents. These wires have to be rated and capable of carrying these high currents – a rating of at least six amps is suitable. This will ensure that the high current wiring will not get hot, voltage drops across such a wire run will be kept to a minimum, and the unit will operate efficiently.

The remainder of the wiring of the unit is simple, using 1 A connecting wire.

SUPPLY FROM
CAR BATTERY

Fig. 3.3 Unit internal wiring.

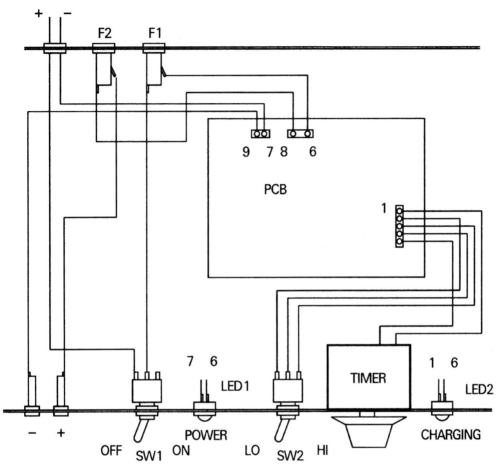

Testing

Once the unit is complete comes the task of testing the charger.

The whole unit can be set up with the aid of the following items; a multimeter able to read 5 A DC, a small LED with a series 1K0 resistor, a 2R2 11 watt (W) wirewound resistor.

First check the PCB for any errors which may have occurred, misplaced components, dry joints, solder bridges, polarity of components etc. Secondly check the internal and external wiring of the charger; this is important because of the high current capacity of a car battery.

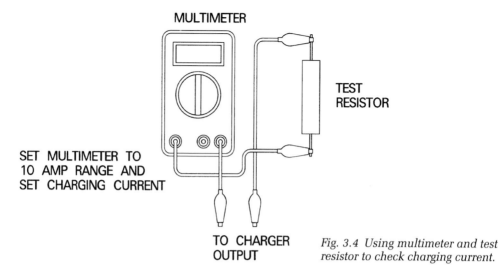

MULTIMETER

TEST
RESISTOR

SET MULTIMETER TO
10 AMP RANGE AND
SET CHARGING CURRENT

TO CHARGER
OUTPUT

Fig. 3.4 Using multimeter and test resistor to check charging current.

The third part of the test procedure is to check the unit powered up and with no charging (nicad) battery connected. Check the current drawn under no load (quiescent) state with a multimeter set to read amps; this should be in the order of 40 mA. When the timer switch is activated the 'charging' LED (LED2) illuminates. The current drawn from the battery should now rise to about 80 mA as the relay is now energised.

With the aid of the test LED and the 1K0 resistor, the function of the pulse generator can now be checked. Connect these components as shown in Figure 3.5, with the anode of the LED connected to the (+12 V) supply of the supply battery, and connect the resistor to pin 3 of IC1 – note that the LED will flash at a rate of ten times a second. The flashing rate will be hard to discern and can only be measured with suitable test equipment, but all that is needed here is to see is that the LED flashes. Connect the resistor now to IC2 pin 6 and note that the LED flashes as before in the initial test at the same rate. If this does not occur,

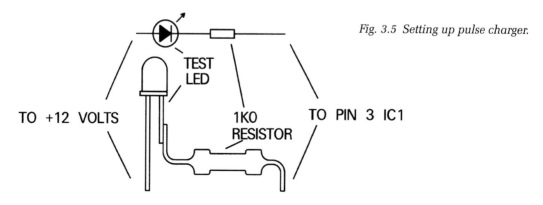

Fig. 3.5 Setting up pulse charger.

TEST
LED

TO +12 VOLTS

1K0
RESISTOR

TO PIN 3 IC1

then adjust Rv1 or Rv2 until the LED does flash. This has now checked out the path of the pulse generator through to the error amplifier circuit.

The constant current generator circuit can now be checked with the use of the 17 W 2R2 as mentioned before. This resistor is connected across the output of the charger, where the charging battery is to be connected, and will get very hot! The current drawn by the unit will rise and is set by Rv1 and Rv2. Rv1 sets the current to 2.5 A, and Rv2, when the switch SW2 is thus selected, draws 2.9 A. This includes the current taken by the 17 W test resistor and the charger circuitry.

Switch off the unit and remove the 17 W 2R2 wirewound resistor from the output sockets of the charger unit once the resistor has cooled down.

Using the charger

The charger is connected to a large storage battery such as a car battery, or any 12–15 V, 3 A DC source.

Connect the battery to be charged to the charger output terminals, and switch on the power switch SW1. This will start trickle charging the battery at about 75 mA. There will be an

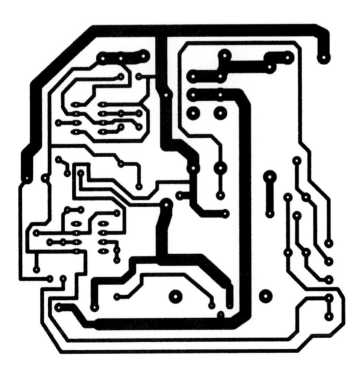

Fig. 3.6 Printed circuit board layout shown from component side (actual size).

additional quiescent current to consider of 40 mA, this will make a total of 115 mA drawn from the storage battery.

To start fast charging the battery, rotate the timer switch, SW3, and the contacts will close; this will run through the charging cycle for thirty minutes and switch off once the charging cycle has been completed. The charger will then return back to trickle charging the battery once the fast charge cycle is completed.

Conclusions

The unit is useful in fast charging sintered cell nicads, and will give a pack a good charge in thirty minutes. Normal nicad battery packs, such as those used in receiver or transmitter battery packs, should not be charged with this unit. They are not capable of venting the volume of gas which can occur when fast charging some nicad cells. The result would most certainly be a small explosion and the battery cell wall would rupture open due to the immense build up of gas which the cell is unable to vent

Component list

R1	12K		C2	10nF
R2	680R		C3	220µF 16V electrolytic
R3	10K		D1	1N4148
R4	10K		D2	IN4001
R5	8K2		D3	1N5401
R6	0R1 3 W wirewound, Maplin stock no: W01R		D4	1N4001
			D5	LED green
R7	10K		D6	LED red
R8	10K		D7	1N4001
R9	100K		LED1	12 V red LED
R10	680R		LED2	12 V red LED
R11	47R 3 W wirewound, Maplin stock no: W47R		TR1	TIP122
Rv1	4K7 preset		IC1	NE555 or LM555
Rv2	4K7 preset		IC2	LM741 or uA741
C1	10µF 16V electrolytic		RLA	SPDT 12V RELAY, Maplin stock no: YX99H

SW1   DPDT 6 A min toggle switch

SW2   SPDT toggle switch

SW3   Clockwork timer switch (0 to 30 mins), available from RS Components (Electromail), stock no: 354-559

Miscellaneous components

■ Case
■ 20 mm 5 A fuses and holders (2 required of each)
■ Heatsink and clip for TR1 (Maplin stock no: AX84F and AX86T)
■ 2R2 17 W wirewound resistor
■ 1K0 ¼ W resistor
■ LED (test)
■ 4 mm terminal (red and black)
■ Nuts, screw, wire etc.

■ 4
Flight Switch with BEC

This flight switch has been designed with a number of features in mind. First, a battery eliminator circuit (BEC) is incorporated. The BEC is a discrete power supply unit which is designed to operate at a low drop out voltage (the difference between the input and output voltage of the voltage regulator), with a sustained current being drawn by the receiver and associated circuitry of 250 mA, and a peak current of just over 1 A. This obviates the need for a receiver nicad battery pack, and the power for the R/C equipment is taken through this BEC circuit.

The second part is the electronic switch circuitry which is capable of switching a sustained motor current of about 15 A maximum.

The final part of the circuit is the section which senses the battery voltage and switches off current supplied through this unit to the model's motor when in flight. This part of the circuit is designed to sense the supply battery voltage and when the battery has discharged sufficiently, cuts out the model's motor. This allows the model to fly and operate the radio control equipment giving flying time to return the model to the ground, but no power to the motor. However, the power to the motor can be shut off at anytime prior to the cut-out coming into effect by command from the transmitter.

The circuit

This project lends a lot of its design work to the low current switch described in Chapter 5. The part of the circuit which discriminates between receiver pulse widths and performs the switching function is similar. However, there is additional circuitry which is incorporated to integrate the extra functions.

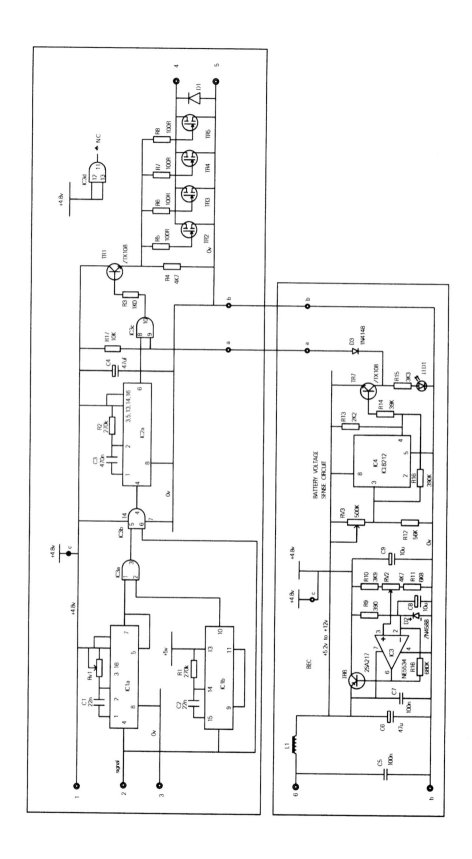

Fig. 4.1 Flight switch with BEC circuit diagram.

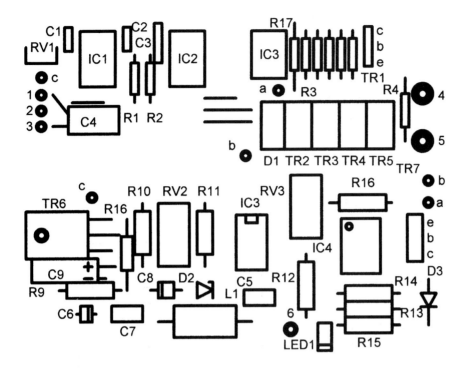

Fig. 4.2 Component layouts for both boards. Top board is shown from track side, bottom board is shown from top side of PCB.

IC4 is a battery monitor integrated circuit and is capable of operating reliably under very low voltages, even down to 3.0 V. This integrated circuit is set up to monitor the voltage of the main motive battery's voltage. Once the model is airborne, and the motor is drawing current from the battery, the battery will then begin to discharge. The effect of the battery discharging is pronounced because the battery voltage begins to fall as a consequence. This fall in voltage is detected by IC4, and when a predetermined voltage has been reached during discharge, IC4 will detect this and signal this response to IC3C at pin 9 via TR7. This will override any effect that the receiver pulse width circuitry has and cut off the power to the model's motor. The remaining flight time is dependent on a number of factors, one – the condition of the batteries, and two – the voltage which the unit is set to cut the motor current off. This is set to approximately 5.5 V, a point where the regulator circuitry is capable of operating correctly.

Construction

The whole circuit is constructed on two PCBs. The smaller board accommodates the main high current switch circuitry, while the second part accommodates the BEC and the voltage detector. The two circuits are linked together via a number of discrete wires. This assists the constructor in making a choice in the final unit i.e. should a BEC be employed within the unit, or indeed should a voltage detector circuit be employed to inhibit the function of the high current switch circuit? The high current switch circuitry will perform without the associated power supply and voltage threshold circuitry, but the power for the circuit has to come from the receiver nicad pack and not through the power supply circuitry. The associated interconnecting wires, a to a, b to b, c to c and the power lead to 6 on the larger board have to be omitted.

Setting up the BEC

Connect the circuit as shown in Figure 4.3 but with one major omission – do not at this point connect any allied radio control circuitry, i.e. the radio control receiver or any other device. Simply switch the power on to the circuit and connect a multimeter set to read DC

Completed BEC and cut-out PCB.

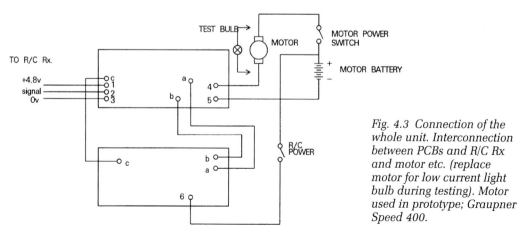

Fig. 4.3 Connection of the whole unit. Interconnection between PCBs and R/C Rx and motor etc. (replace motor for low current light bulb during testing). Motor used in prototype; Graupner Speed 400.

voltage at points 'b' and 'c' on the power supply board. Adjust Rv2 until the voltage read on the multimeter is 4.8 V.

Setting up the battery voltage sense circuit

The BEC is simply set up. First, disconnect any source of power to the circuit. Remove IC4, measure the resistance with the aid of a multimeter across the pins 3 and 8 of the socket, adjust Rv3 until the resistance measured is about 390 K. Replace IC4.

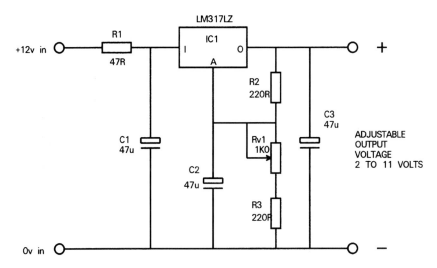

Fig. 4.4 Test power supply.

Setting up (the switch)

The setting up for the actual semiconductor switch part is included for this project, and is similar to the low current switch set-up described elsewhere in the book, but with a few differences and additions. The additions are included because of the extra circuitry employed in the BEC and the voltage sensing cut-out circuit. See Figure 4.3. At this stage use a test light bulb rated at the voltage of the motor in place of the motor.

Connect the unit to an appropriate channel on a receiver output. Set up the system with the transmitter and receiver working.

It is an advantage to know which positions on the transmitter joystick correspond to the shorter and longer pulse width coming from the receiver servo output. This helps in setting up the switch.

A multimeter set to read 1.0 V DC full scale is connected to the receiver servo output –

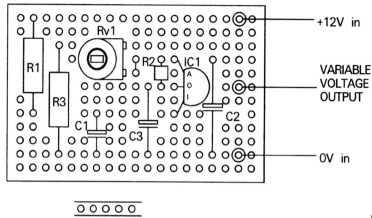

COPPER STRIPS RUN HORIZONTALLY

Fig. 4.5 Construction of test power supply on stripboard.

monitor the voltage at this point. Move the joystick back and forth. Note the reading on the multimeter at each extreme on the joystick. The greater the pulse width the higher the voltage; this would read somewhere in the region of 250 mV or a quarter of a volt maximum.

With the unit connected to the receiver servo output, set the preset Rv1, to mid position. Put a test load, i.e. a light bulb as shown in Figure 4.3 and move the joystick from the position where the pulse width measured is at its least. Adjust Rv1 until the light extinguishes, move the joystick to the other extreme, where the pulse width is at its longest. The light should now illuminate. If this does not occur adjust Rv1 until the action of the joystick operates the light.

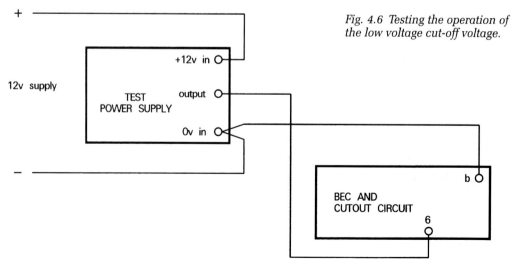

Fig. 4.6 Testing the operation of the low voltage cut-off voltage.

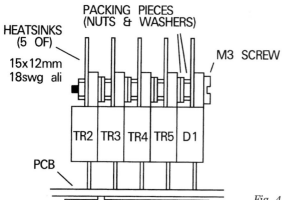

Fig. 4.7 *Mounting of the power transistors and D1.*

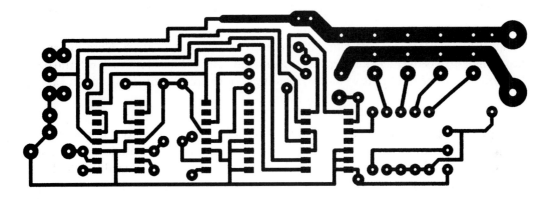

Fig. 4.8 *Layout shown from top side of board (switch board) (twice actual size).*

Fig. 4.9 *Layout shown from component (top) side of PCB (twice actual size).*

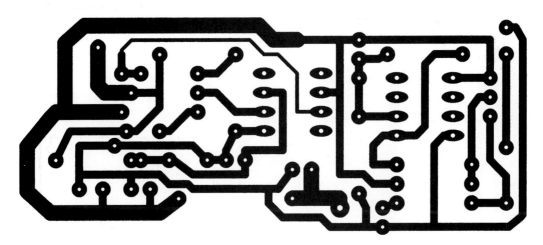

Should the unit be attached to a channel where a switch is used on the transmitter, the switch is switched back and forth to determine the maximum pulse width and the switching point of the unit.

Setting up – checking operation of cut-out circuit

Make a test power supply as shown in Figure 4.4. This will confirm the setting up of the voltage sense circuit. Connect it up to a 12 V supply, such as a twelve volt lead acid battery, and adjust Rv1 of the power supply to set the trigger voltage of the sense circuit. Set the test power supply output voltage to 5.5 V in this example simulating a six cell battery. Use a multimeter to set the output voltage of the test power supply. Connect the power supply to pins 6 and 'b' of the flight switch, observing the correct polarity. Adjust Rv1 on the test power supply until the on-board indicator LED1 extinguishes – this should be just below 5.5 V. Adjusting Rv1 on the test power supply will bring the voltage back up on the test power supply to 6.5 V, thus simulating the operation in flight of the load being removed from the motive battery, i.e. the motor being switched off, and the on -board indicator LED1 remaining off. The LED on the cut-out circuitry should not illuminate again until the test power supply voltage reaches 7.0 V or more.

Connecting up

The operation of the whole circuit is best checked using a low current component such as a light bulb in place of a high current electric motor. Connect the circuit as shown in Figure 4.3.

Completed switch and interconnections of both PCBs (prototype). Note D3 – mounted off board.

Note

Once this circuit is set up in the model it is wise to complete a test run and time the length of the model's flight on the bench, and satisfactory operation of the radio control equipment once the motor has cut out. Check also for satisfactory operation of all the servos for a number of minutes after the motor has cut out. This will simulate the flight and the model landing.

Components list

R1	270K	C5	100n
R2	270K	C6	47μF 16V PCB mounting electrolytic
R3	1K0	C7	100n
R4	1K0	C8	10μF 16V PCB mounting electrolytic
R5	100R	C9	10μF 16V PCB mounting electrolytic
R6	100R	L1	100μH choke
R7	100R	TR1	ZTX108
R8	100R	TR2	BUK555GDA
R9	390R	TR3	BUK555GDA
R10	3K9	TR4	BUK555GDA
R11	6K8	TR5	BUK555GDA
R12	56K	TR6	2SA715
R13	47K	TR7	ZTX108
R14	39K	LED1	3 mm LED
R15	3K3	D1	SK820
R16	680K	D2	ZN428B
R17	10K	IC1	HEF4528BT surface mount, Farnell part no: 387-381
Rv1	470K preset		
Rv2	5K0 preset 10 turn	IC2	HEF4528BT surface mount
Rv3	500K preset 10 turn	IC3	HEF4081BT surface mount, Farnell part no: 387-241
C1	22n		
C2	22n	IC4	NE5534
C3	470n	IC5	ICL8212
C4	47μF 16V PCB mounting electrolytic		

Miscellaneous components

■ Interconnecting wire
■ Terminal pins, etc

Test circuit

R1	47R		C1	47µF 16V PCB mounting electrolytic
R2	220R		C2	47µF 16V PCB mounting electrolytic
R3	220R		IC1	LM317Z adjustable voltage regulator
Rv1	1K0			

Miscellaneous components

■ Stripboard
■ Tinned copper wire
■ Terminal pins, etc.

■ 5
Low Current Switch

This simple unit described here is designed to remotely operate low current devices such as landing lights on a model aircraft. The switch is rated at a maximum current of approximately 2.0 A. The unit is remotely operated from the transmitter and is connected within the model to an appropriate receiver channel.

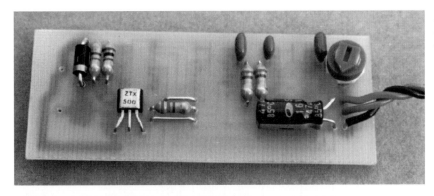

Low current switch top side of PCB.

Low power switch track side.

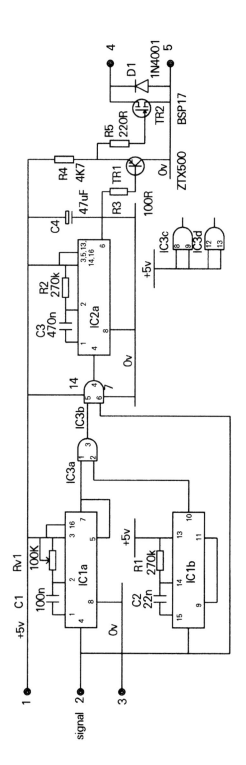

Fig. 5.1 Low current switch circuit diagram.

The circuit

The switch circuit consists of three monostables – IC1a, IC1b and IC2a. The receiver servo output signal is fed to the input of both IC1a and IC1b, and power is also taken from the receiver to operate the switch. The pulse width modulated signal from the receiver triggers both these monostables, IC1a and IC1b. The first monostable triggers and remains on for a period of about 1.4 ms, the actual value is determined by the setting of Rv1. The second monostable which triggers at the same time remains on for a period of approximately 2.5 ms.

From the two monostables, IC1a and IC1b, the outputs are both fed to an AND gate IC2a, and from the output of this gate a delayed pulse of 1.10 ms width is produced. The delay is set by the period of the first monostable IC1a, which in this case is approximately 1.4 ms. The resultant pulse width is the difference in timing of the two monostables IC1a and IC1b. The output of the AND gate is compared with the incoming pulse from the receiver, and from the second AND gate (IC2b) an output is either generated or not. The presence or absence of this pulse will depend on the width of the pulse coming from the radio control receiver.

Two cases exist; (1) where the pulse width from the receiver is less than 1.4 ms (the timing period of IC1a), and (2) where the pulse width from the receiver is greater than 1.4 ms. Considering the case in (1) above, when the pulse width is less than 1.4 ms there will be no output from the AND gate IC3b. When the pulse width is lengthened to a value greater than the value set at the first monostable IC1a, an output pulse (signal) is generated to trigger the last monostable IC3a.

The period of the third monostable is set to a value which is much greater than the pulse width repetition rate being sent from the radio control receiver, which in most cases is about 20 ms. The timing period of the third monostable is set to about 50 ms. Every time the pulse width is greater than 1.4mS the third monostable will be constantly triggered

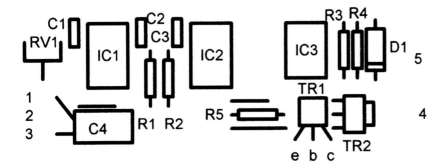

Fig. 5.2 Component layout shown from track side.

thus keeping the output of this third monostable in a high logic state, the output of which feeds TR1, an emitter follower and then on to the main switching transistor TR2. D1 is provided to protect the switching transistor TR2.

Construction

The unit is constructed on a single sided PCB, the integrated circuits IC1, IC2, IC3 and the transistor TR2 are all surface mount components and are mounted on the track side of the board. The remainder are mounted on the top side of the board. All the components which are mounted on the top side of the board are mounted as close to the board as possible, they can be stuck to that side with a small spot of glue. These are C1, C2, C3, C4 and TR1. This will help the circuit to withstand impact damage.

Setting up

Connect the unit to an appropriate channel on a receiver output. Set up the system with the transmitter and receiver working.

It is an advantage to know which positions on the transmitter joystick correspond to the shorter and longer pulse width coming from the receiver servo output. This helps in setting up the switch.

A multimeter set to read 1.0 V DC full scale is connected to the receiver servo output – monitor the voltage at this point. Move the joystick back and forth. Note the reading on the multimeter at each extreme on the joystick. The greater the pulse width the higher the voltage – this would read somewhere in the region of 250 mV or a quarter of a volt.

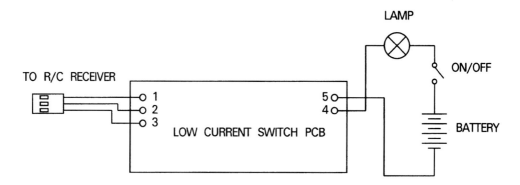

Fig. 5.3 Example of connecting circuit to lamp (landing light).

With the unit connected to the receiver servo output, set the preset Rv1, to mid position. Put a test load, i.e. a light bulb as shown in Figure 5.3 and move the joystick from the position where the pulse width measured is at its least. Adjust Rv1 until the light extinguishes, move the joystick to the other extreme, where the pulse width is at its longest. The light should now illuminate. If this does not occur adjust Rv1 until the action of the joystick operates the light.

Should the unit be attached to a channel where a switch is used on the transmitter, the switch is switched back and forth to determine the maximum pulse width and the switching point of the unit.

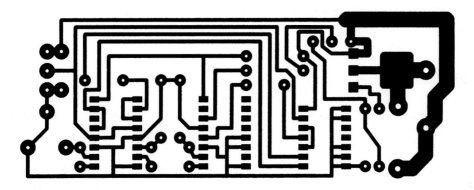

Fig. 5.4 PCB tracks shown from top side of PCB (twice actual size).

In use

The unit is a simple device and performs the function of a single pole single throw (SPST) switch. It can therefore be utilised to switch for example a landing light on, a relay or a sound effects device. The unit can replace what would otherwise utilise a servo and a small slide switch. The maximum current drawn from the receiver battery is minimal and should not add too much of a drain from the receiver battery. The maximum current drawn through the switch part of the circuit is at a maximum of some two amps. A fuse can be accommodated in the model which is in series with the battery and the device being switched.

Components list

R1	270K		R4	4K7
R2	270K		R5	220R
R3	100R		Rv1	100K preset

C1	100n	IC2	HEF4528BT surface mount
C2	22n	IC3	HEF4081BT surface mount, Farnell part no: 387-241
C3	470n		
C4	47u 16V PCB mounting electrolytic	TR1	ZTX500
IC1	HEF4528BT surface mount, Farnell part no: 387-381	TR2	BSP17 surface mount FET, surface mount, Farnell BSP17
		D1	1N4001

Miscellaneous components

- PCB
- Wire
- Terminal pins

■ 6
Receiver Nicad Battery Tester

Prior to a model's flight it is useful to check the condition of its receiver nicad pack – even to check the battery pack is in a charged state after an overnight charge. This unit is designed to check a standard 4.8 V receiver nicad pack, and give you a go/no go state of charge.

Receiver nicad tester.

As discussed elsewhere in this book, the state of charge of a battery can be ascertained from sampling the voltage of the battery under test when using a load current. This unit has the facility to check a 4.8 V nicad pack under a load current of approximately 150 mA.

This unit is set to trigger at a preset threshold, and is set at a point where it is considered the battery when charged would be 50% charged or indeed higher. The 'fail' indicator will illuminate and indicate a discharged battery should the battery voltage be lower during the test.

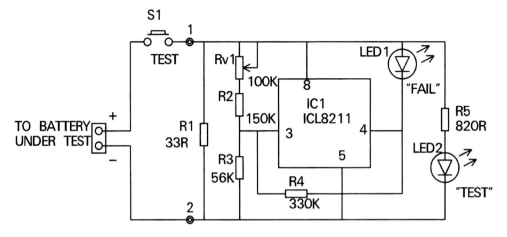

Fig. 6.1 Simple receiver nicad battery tester circuit diagram.

The circuit

The circuit for the nicad tester is designed around the ICL8211 voltage detector integrated circuit, the reason being that this device will operate over a wide voltage range, up to 30 V, and down to an incredible 3 V – ideal for this application. The chip is designed to operate on battery powered equipment and is very well suited, drawing a minute amount of current from the attached circuit.

The unit is battery powered and takes its power from the battery under test. The integrated circuit IC1 is a device which has a precision voltage reference source of 1.15 V. IC1 compares the sample taken from the potential divider R2 and R3 and Rv1 at pin 3 of IC1. This

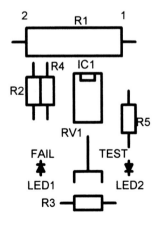

Fig. 6.2 Component layout.

sample voltage is compared to that of the internal voltage reference source of IC1. Should the sampled voltage at pin 3 be higher than the internal chip's reference voltage then the output of IC1 will be high, and LED1 will not illuminate. Lower sampled voltage (at pin 3) – and the output of IC1 pin 4 will fall causing current to flow through LED1 indicating a low sample voltage battery, i.e. fail condition, or discharged battery. The output from IC1 pin 4 is current limited to 7 mA, which is sufficient to illuminate the indicator LED1 without the need of a current limiting resistor which would otherwise be required. R4 is included in the circuit to introduce hysteresis – this reduces switching problems that could otherwise occur and gives a clean indication of the switching point.

LED2 is included to show that the unit is operating and in use. Should the 'test' (LED2) indicator illuminate and the fail indicator remain unlit during the test procedure then all is well and the battery being tested is charged.

R1 is included to load the battery under test. This component can be omitted should the unit be installed permanently in a model, and the receiver, servos and allied circuitry providing the test load current. LED 2 can also be omitted if desired. With the unit permanently installed in a model additionally R1, R5 and LED2 can also be omitted. The unit will function taking only a minute amount of power from the model's nicad pack, and not significantly affecting the amount of flight time.

Setting up

The unit is set up using the following guide.

Connect the unit to a charged battery. Measure the voltage across the battery or R1 with the aid of a multimeter and take note of this voltage. Now monitor the voltage across R3.

Using the following formula:

$$\text{Voltage across R3} = \frac{\text{Battery voltage}}{3.72}$$

adjust Rv1 until the voltage on the multimeter reads the calculated value from the formula above. This will set the threshold of the battery fail condition to an approximate battery charge of 50%.

Check out the circuit with a charged 4.8 V nicad battery pack. Connect the nicad tester to a load resistor as shown in Figure 6.4, then connect the circuit to the receiver pack. Observe the two indicators on the circuit. The 'test' indicator (LED2) should remain illuminated

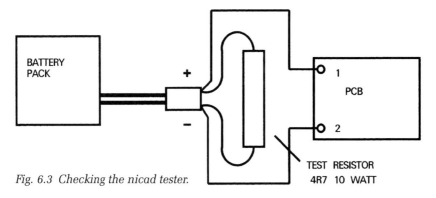

Fig. 6.3 Checking the nicad tester.

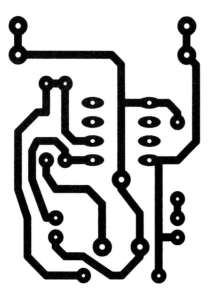

Fig. 6.4 PCB layout shown through from component side (twice actual size).

throughout the test. Take a note of the time taken for the 'fail' indicator (LED1) to illuminate, and observe the voltage across the load resistor. The time taken for the battery to discharge should be about twenty minutes, and the battery voltage should have fallen to no less than 4.28 V. Below this point the radio control receiver and servo circuitry could otherwise fail.

As a guideline, setting the preset Rv1 at the 4 o'clock position would be an approximate setting for this control, and triggers the fail condition at 4.28 V.

Component list

R1	33R, 1 W carbon film		IC1	ICL8211
R2	150K		S1	momentary action push to make SPST switch
R3	56K			
R4	330K		LED1	LED
R5	820R		LED2	LED
Rv1	100K preset, Maplin stock no: UH06G			

Miscellaneous components

- PCB
- Wire
- Connectors
- Case
- Terminal pins
- Test resistor 4R7 10 watt wirewound Maplin stock no: H4R7.

■ 7
Tachometer

Measuring a model's propeller speed is essential if optimum performance from the model is desired. The use of a tachometer is the prescribed piece of equipment used to measure the engine speed of a model. The tachometer described here is designed to operate with model aircraft using two or three bladed propellers, the type of propeller is selected with the aid of a switch mounted on the self-contained battery powered unit. The reading of the engine speed is given numerically on a liquid crystal display (LCD). In use the unit is positioned in front of the rotating propeller, and relies on the reflected infrared light beam sent from an infrared emitter and received back at the unit from the rotating propeller, thus providing a series of pulses which are proportional to the engine speed. Further processing is required to convert these received pulses to some numeric form – this is described later.

Completed PCB (tachometer).

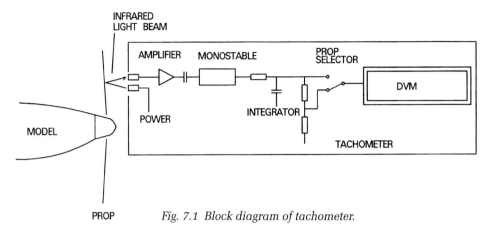

Fig. 7.1 Block diagram of tachometer.

The circuit described here is a tachometer designed to monitor the speed of a propeller, running up to a maximum speed of 20,000 rpm.

The circuit

The technique used here to measure the rotational speed of a model's propeller is one which is commonly used. As shown in Figure 7.1, the technique of using a reflected infrared (IR) beam from the unit is employed.

When the unit is used to ascertain the propeller speed it is positioned two inches in front of the rotating propeller. The push button switch SW1 is depressed which supplies power to the circuit. Power is supplied from the unit's integral PP3 alkaline nine volt battery. The infrared diode D1 (diode current is approximately 80 mA) fires forward an IR light beam along the axis of the diode, strikes the blade of the rotating propeller and is then instantly reflected back to the unit. This reflected light is received by the IR receiver IC1. Within this unit is an IR detector and amplifier stage. This integral amplifier boosts the signal received by the IR diode integrated within the unit. The signal is further amplified by a second amplifier IC2. This amplifier is AC coupled, and will reduce any spurious infrared emissions on the field. TR1 and TR2 provide a voltage level conversion which is suitable to trigger the monostable IC3.

Each time the monostable IC3 is triggered with the passing of the propeller blade, the output pulse from IC3 remains in a logic 'hi' state for a preset time; this is determined by the associated timing components of IC3, C3 and Rv1.

Following the monostable is a half wave rectifier D3 which charges C6 through R11. R12 and R13 form a potential divider which is used to divide the voltage across the capacitor

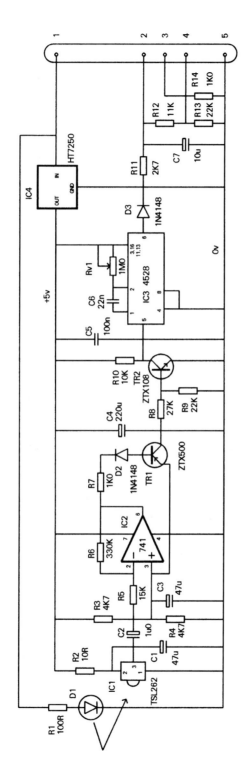

Fig. 7.2 Circuit diagram.

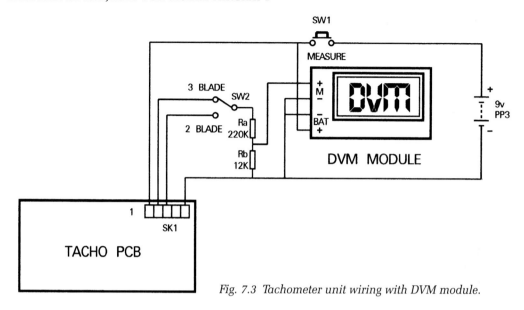

Fig. 7.3 Tachometer unit wiring with DVM module.

C6 and give the desired range setting for two and three bladed propellers to be read by the DVM module indicating the propeller speed.

In use, the monostable and rectifier circuit have the following purpose. Assuming a two bladed propeller, consider the following condition; the monostable is being triggered at two hundred times a second (6,000 rpm) and charging the capacitor C6, with a trigger signal from the model's propeller. C6 will be charged at a fast rate through R11 and discharge slowly through R12 and R13, by virtue of their relative resistance values. This is due to R11 being much smaller in value than the series combination of R12 and R13. This will allow C6 to charge up, and the average voltage reached by C6 will be determined by three factors as follows: the peak voltage of the charging pulse from the monostable IC3, the pulse width from IC3, and the rate at which the monostable is triggered. Since the pulse width and peak voltage is set, the only remaining variable is the trigger rate of the monostable. When the monostable trigger frequency is raised, as the propeller revolves faster, for example, to four hundred times a second (12,000 rpm), the capacitor C6 will charge up to twice the previous voltage, thus producing a linear relationship between the rate at which the monostable is triggered and the output voltage of the circuit. Hence the rotational speed of a propeller in this specific situation. This DC voltage is fed to a device which reads DC voltage, in this example a digital volt meter (DVM). This is calibrated to read voltage and gives a numerical display of the propeller's speed.

Alternative to LCD module

An alternative to the use of an LCD module as a means to display the propeller speed is the use of a moving coil meter. This is used in place of the DVM module and is wired as shown in Figure 7.6. R14 is used in this circumstance and is soldered into the PCB. Calibration follows a similar procedure laid down for the DVM module, the only difference being the speed is read from the calibrated meter scale.

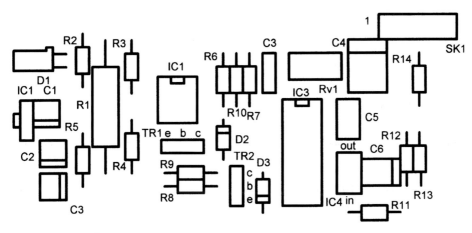

Fig. 7.4 Component layout.

Construction

The project is constructed on one PCB, and mounted in a hand-held enclosure. Provision is made in the enclosure for the infrared components to operate, two holes 6 mm diameter are cut and these are ample sized windows for each of the infrared devices. The DVM module is mounted on the enclosure as shown completing the unit.

External wiring to the board is accomplished to the range switch SW2 and the power switch SW1, and additionally to the DVM module, or the moving coil movement.

Calibration of the unit

To ensure the unit gives an accurate reading the pulse width produced by the monostable IC3 has to be adjusted. In this way the tachometer can be calibrated and indicate accurate readings.

Most people will be familiar with infrared hand-held remote controllers for videos, television sets, hifi units and a lot more. They seem to be ever more used in the domestic world for a variety of things. A trick can be demonstrated with a domestic remote controller of holding the controller in the right hand, holding the emitter part close up to the palm of the left hand and firing the infrared source through the hand to control a television set. In most cases the experiment would have to be completed close to the unit being controlled – within a couple of inches.

Normal domestic filament light bulbs running on AC, despite running at 50 Hz, will flicker at twice this rate, a hundred times a second. They tend to emit a large amount of energy, some in the form of light, the remainder in the infrared spectrum in the form of heat. This is emitted across a broad spectrum too. The mains frequency is closely regulated, and can be relied on to provide a stable means of a timebase to calibrate the unit.

By combining the two techniques shown it is possible to calibrate the unit, using the light as a broad band light source, and the hand as an infrared filter.

The set-up for calibrating the unit is shown in the photograph. The unit is laid open and switched on. A small screwdriver is used to set the reading on the DVM module by rotat-

Calibrating the tachometer unit.

ing the control on Rv1. Switch on the light source, an angle poise lamp with a 60 W bulb will suffice, and ensure the lamp is about ten inches from the unit. Place your hand in front of the unit, about two inches from the infrared detector – your hand will absorb the majority of the visible light and pass through a portion of infrared to which the detector is also sensitive. A warning – the light bulb will get hot during use, and a degree of caution is advised. Note that the reading on the DVM will rise as your hand is placed in front of the light. Adjust the preset Rv1 until the DVM reads 30 mV, this indicating 3,000 rpm. For use in the US, and countries where the mains power distribution is different, for example 60 Hz AC, adjust the preset Rv1 until the reading shows 36, indicating 3,600 rpm.

Use of the tachometer

The tachometer is used as shown in Figure 7.5. First, the prop blade is selected, either two or three as appropriate for the propeller. The unit is then activated by depressing SW1 allowing the unit to become active and capable of measuring propeller speed. It is positioned approximately one to two inches from the model's rotating propeller, midway from the axis of the motor to the tip of the prop. Any closer in to the boss of the prop and an inaccurate reading would be obtained. The unit can be operated from this midway point outwards with no loss in accuracy of the unit.

A word of warning, do not look directly into the infrared emitting diode of this unit or, for that matter, any remote control device. The invisible light coming from these units is of a high level and may cause damage to eyes if subjected to prolonged misuse.

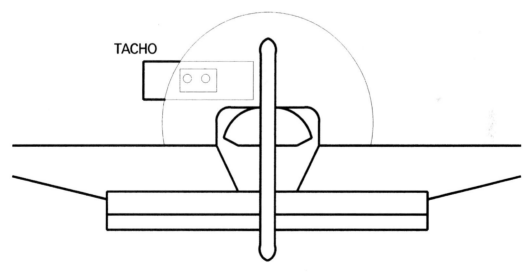

Fig. 7.5 Position of hand-held tachometer reading prop speed. IR light beam should illuminate part of the prop greater than halfway along prop blade in use.

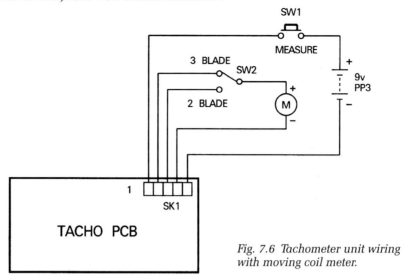

Fig. 7.6 Tachometer unit wiring with moving coil meter.

List of components

R1	100R 2 W
R2	10R
R3	4K7
R4	4K7
R5	15K
R6	330K
R7	1K0
R8	27K
R9	22K
R10	10K
R11	2K7
R12	11K
R13	22K
R14	see text, if required, 1K0
C1	47µF 16V PCB mounting electrolytic
C2	1u0 63V PCB mounting electrolytic
C3	47µF 16V PCB mounting electrolytic

C4	220µF 25V PCB mounting electrolytic
C5	100nF
C6	22nF
C7	10µF 25V PCB mounting electrolytic
D1	Infrared emitting diode, TIL38, Maplin stock no: YH70M
D2	1N4148
D3	1N4148
TR1	ZTX500
TR2	ZTX108
IC1	TSL262, Farnell stock no: 460-941
IC2	NE5534
IC3	4529 or 4098
IC4	HT7250 5 V 100mA voltage regulator, Maplin stock no: LE79L
DVM	DVM module, Maplin stock no: GW01B

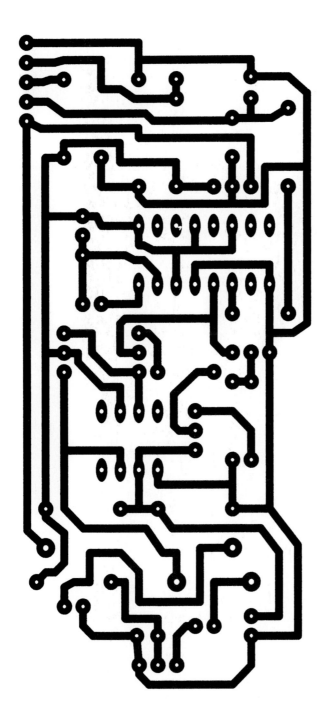

Fig. 7.7 PCB track layout shown through from component side (twice actual size).

Miscellaneous components

- PCB
- Connecting wire
- SPDT switch
- PTM push button switch
- 8 and 16 pin DIL sockets
- 5 way PCB mounting socket and mating plug, and connectors
- PP3 style battery and clip, enclosure, etc.
- Moving coil meter 50uA movement Maplin stock no: FM98G (alternative to DVM module).

Additional components for DVM

Ra   220K (20,000 rpm)

Rb   12K

■ 8
Nicad Battery Discharger

When using nicad batteries a certain amount of care has to be exercised. The use of rechargeable nicad battery packs is almost universal in electric flight models as the battery can be charged, used and recharged again ready for another flight within an hour.

One known problem with nicad batteries is the so-called memory effect. This phenomena causes a problem primarily where a battery is discharged and not discharged fully, thus

Nicad battery discharger.

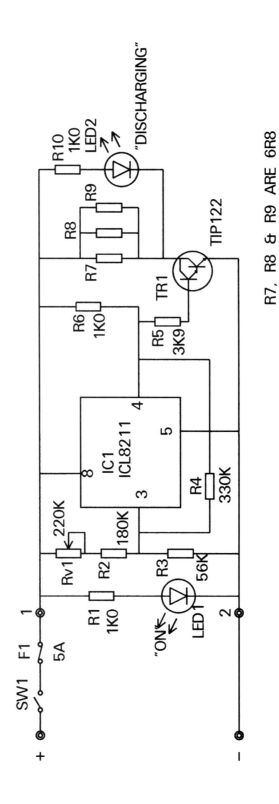

Fig. 8.1 Nicad battery discharger circuit diagram.

leaving a residual charge within the battery. For example, there could be a 20% charge remaining in the battery after use. When the battery is charged again, taking 80% charge (in effect topping it up), the memory effect has the consequence of reducing the effective charge in this example shown to 80%, thus losing 20% or one-fifth of the total capacity of the battery. The memory effect occurs when repeated charging and topping up of the battery as described is carried out.

The way to avoid this problem is to discharge the battery approximately 95% each time the battery has been used. If the battery is used in a model and returned to the ground after flight, there should be a residual charge remaining. This residual charge can be reduced such that it is eliminated before another charge of the battery is undertaken.

It would be detrimental to the battery to just uncontrollably dump the residual charge from the battery. What has also to be considered is the effect of dumping the residual charge and leaving the battery discharged. This could have the effect of discharging the battery totally resulting in the possibility that it will be unable to recover to be recharged ever again.

The circuit described here is designed to discharge nicad packs, and switch off the discharge cycle, leaving a minute charge in the battery prior to the battery being charged again ready for flight.

The circuit

The heart of the circuit is the versatile ICL8211 battery monitor integrated circuit. It is a useful device which is specifically designed for use in battery powered equipment. The ICL8211 (IC1) is configured as a comparator with additional hysterisis provided by R4. This operates as a switch turning on or off the load which is provided by three power resistors R7, R8 and R9 via the Darlington pair transistor TR1. The dump current is in the order of 2 to 3 A, this depending on the actual battery pack voltage.

IC1 senses the voltage presented at pin 3. If this is higher than 1.15 V then the output at pin 4 will be high, turning on the power transistor TR1, providing a path for current to flow through the load resistors. When the sensed voltage at pin 3 of IC1 falls below 1.15 V, then the output voltage at pin 4 of IC1 falls switching off the power to the load resistors dumping power from the battery. The circuit will only then take a minute amount of current from the discharged battery.

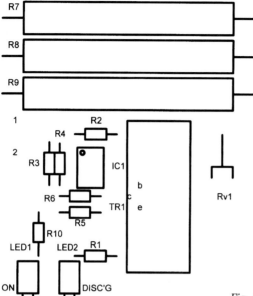

Fig. 8.2 Component layout.

Construction

The construction of the circuit is straightforward, but account is taken of some of the components getting hot during the discharge cycle, namely the three power resistors R7, R8 and R9. The power transistor which is heatsinked will dissipate some heat, but should be small in comparison to the load resistors. Therefore the load resistors have to be mounted clear of the PCB to avoid scorching the board when in use. A clearance of about 3 mm for ventilation should be sufficient. The leads of the load resistors can be bent as shown in Figure 8.3, as a means of securing the component and ensuring the component is clear of the board.

BEND LEADS AS SHOWN, ALLOWING 3mm OF SPACE BETWEEN RESISTOR AND PCB (THIS ALLOWS AIR TO CIRCULATE AROUND THE RESISTOR)

Fig. 8.3 Mounting of the power load resistors.

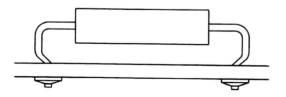

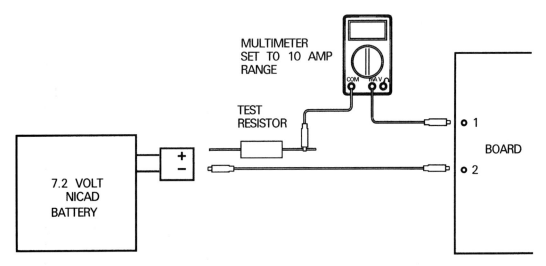

MULTIMETER
SET TO 10 AMP
RANGE

TEST
RESISTOR

BOARD

o 1

o 2

7.2 VOLT
NICAD
BATTERY

+
−

Fig. 8.4 Checking the discharging current during testing.

The unit is mounted in an enclosure, and adequate ventilation has to be provided to enable the heat dissipated in the power transistor and the load resistors to be carried away from the circuitry.

Setting up

The unit requires the following setting-up procedure. Connect the completed unit as shown in Figure 8.4 with a series connected test 10 Ω 10 W wirewound resistor. With the aid of a multimeter connected to measure current in circuit (i.e. set to 10 A current range) measure the current with the unit switched on. This should in the region of half an amp (500 mA). Remove the 10 Ω wirewound test resistor from the test circuit shown, and measure the current drawn in the discharge mode again. The reading should be in the region of 2½ A for a charged 7.2 V nicad pack and up to three and a half amps for a 9.6 volt nicad pack. Setting the preset potentiometer Rv1 to the one o'clock position will give a switch off voltage of approximately 4.8 V, with an additional 3 V hysteresis, which means the circuit will not again draw any appreciable current when it has switched off until the battery voltage, or the supplied voltage rises above 8 V.

In use

To use the unit is simplicity itself. Connect the battery to be discharged to the unit, switch the unit on – LED1 and LED2 should both illuminate. This will show that the battery is charged and is supplying current to the circuit and power is being dumped into the power resistors. When the unit has reached a sufficient level to discharge the battery to approximately five volts, LED2 will extinguish but LED1 will remain lit. The action of LED2 extinguishing will indicate the battery has been discharged sufficiently to be disconnected. LED1 remaining lit indicates the battery is still connected, but no current is being dumped into the circuit. A residual current will be drawn by the circuit to supply power to illuminate LED1 – approximately 5 mA. The battery connected to the unit should lose its residual charge in some ten minutes connected to this unit, although this will largely depend on the depth of discharge of the battery connected to the unit. The battery is immediately removed from the unit after discharge and recharged.

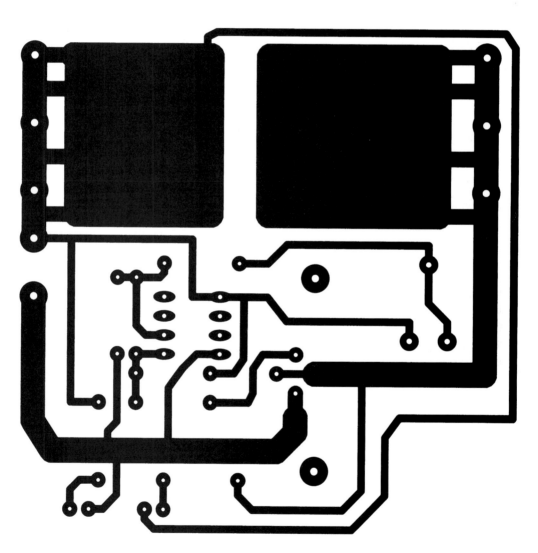

Fig. 8.5 PCB track shown through component side (twice actual size).

The circuit is rated to run at with a maximum of 8 nicad cells. The limit is set by the total power dissipated in the three load resistors R7, R8 and R9.

It is recommended that the unit is operated under constant supervision conditions, and that it is not left running overnight – damage could result to the battery pack being discharged.

Component list

R1	1K0		R9	6R8 11 W wire-ended wirewound resistor
R2	180K		R10	1K0
R3	56K		Rv1	220K preset, Maplin stock no: UH07H
R4	330K		TR1	TIP122
R5	3K9		LED1	PCB mounting LED
R6	1K0		LED2	PCB mounting LED
R7	6R8 11 W wire-ended wirewound resistor		IC1	ICL8211
R8	6R8 11 W wire-ended wirewound resistor		F1	5A 20mm fuse

Miscellaneous components

- Fuse holder
- PCB
- Switch
- Terminal pins
- Wire etc.

■ 9

Electric Motor Speed Controller

The speed of an electric motor in a model can be controlled remotely from the ground. In this project the familiar ZN409CE integrated circuit manufactured by Ferranti used in many servo and speed controller designs is used again here. With other designs the speed controller has been used with a function to reverse the rotation of the motor. In this application this has not been incorporated in this design as it was thought unnecessary.

Completed speed controller.

The circuit

The motor speed controller is based on the Ferranti servo driver chip which, in this application, is arranged as a speed controller rather than in its more familiar role of actuating a servo.

69

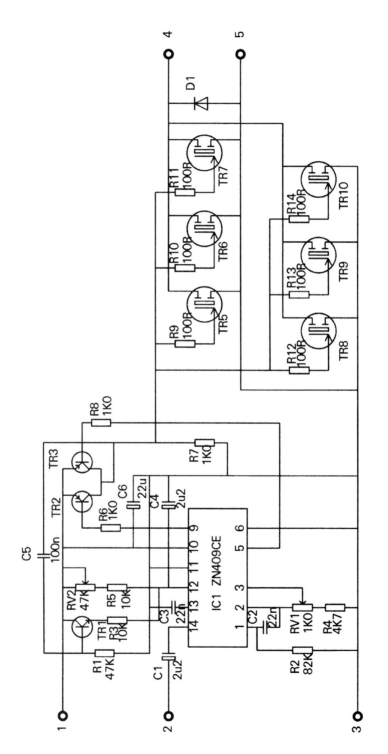

Fig. 9.1 Circuit diagram.

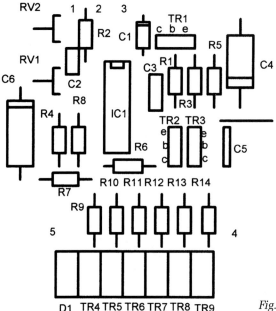

Fig. 9.2 Component layout.

The main function of IC1, ZN409CE, is to process the incoming PWM signal from the receiver servo output port and to act as a linear pulse width amplifier. This then in turn drives the power FETs which, in turn, drive the motor with a series of pulses whose width is determined by the width of the incoming signal from the receiver servo port. The mark/space ratio is varied, and the motor speed accordingly. The result of this is that when the receiver pulse is longer, the corresponding speed of the motor is faster and, conversely, the shorter the pulse, the slower the motor rotates.

Construction

The circuit is constructed on a PCB with all the components mounted on the top side. The six power FETs are mounted as shown, and can be attached to an aluminium heatsink to reduce the temperature rise in these components. The protection diode D1 is also attached to the heatsink. Some PCB tracks will be taking high motor currents, so it is therefore advisable to build up the tracks with extra solder to make the track paths a lower resistance and thus more capable of handling the high currents on the PCB. The power FETs and D1 are mounted last of all, these seven components being secured to the heatsink and the PCB with a long M3 screw, or studding. A good means of providing thermal conductivity from the power FETs to the heatsink is to smear a small amount of heatsink compound to the underside of each power FET and D1. This will help conduct heat generated in these power devices away to the heatsink and keep those devices cooler.

Setting up

The unit is connected as shown in Figure 9.3. Make sure the connections to the board and from the receiver are correct. Once you are satisfied that the test circuit is correctly wired, switch on the receiver battery pack, also the transmitter. Measure the voltage present with the aid of a multimeter between pins 3 and 1 on the PCB. This should be the voltage of the receiver battery pack, for a four cell nicad pack this should be around 4.8 V. Connect the supply to the bulb side of the circuit. The bulb may illuminate at this stage but this will depend on the setting of the transmitter joystick and the setting of Rv1 and Rv2. Initially adjust Rv1 and Rv2 to the six o'clock and seven o'clock positions respectively.

The current drawn by the controller from the receiver nicad battery pack should be no greater than 40 mA.

Set the transmitter joystick to a position where use of the control will dictate the motor 'off' position. Then adjust the preset potentiometer Rv1 such that the bulb shown in the test circuit extinguishes. Move the transmitter joystick to the opposite end of its travel – the bulb should now glow bright.

Adjusting Rv2 will now set the maximum brightness of the bulb, and hence when installed in the model, the maximum speed of the model's motor.

The final part of checking the controller is to substitute the model's motor for the bulb. Ensure that an adequately rated fuse is used to cope with the motor current drawn during these tests.

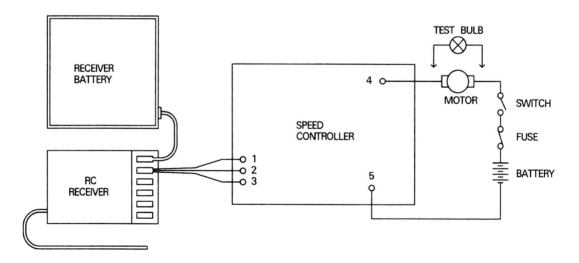

Fig. 9.3 Setting up of the speed controller circuit. Motor used in prototype; Graupner Speed 400.

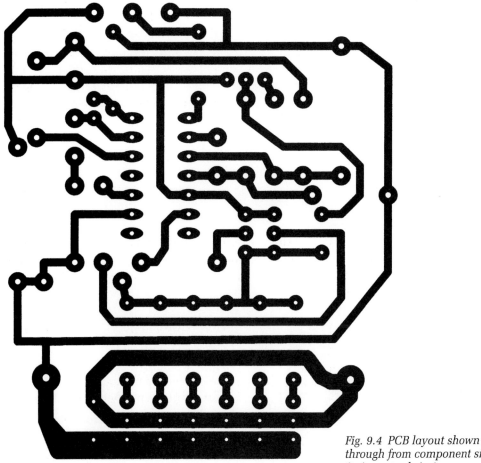

Fig. 9.4 PCB layout shown through from component side (twice actual size).

Connecting the speed controller

This type of speed controller is designed to operate with high current electric motors. All the components associated with the high current paths have to be rated accordingly. Use appropriately rated connecting wire and build up the high current paths on the PCB track side. This will ensure that resistance paths which carry the motor current from the battery through the controller and onto the motor, see the lowest resistance path resulting in a maximum current transfer. The controller will take a maximum current of ten amps.

Component list

R1	47K		C1	2u2 25V axial electrolytic
R2	82K		C2	22n polyester
R3	10K		C3	22n polyester
R4	4K7		C4	2u2 25V axial electrolytic
R5	10K		C5	100n polyester
R6	1K0		C6	22u 25V axial electrolytic
R7	1KO		D1	SK820
R8	1KO		TR1	ZTX108
R9	100R		TR2	ZTX500
R10	100R		TR3	ZTX500
R11	100R		TR4	BUK555-60A, Farnell stock no: 435-041
R12	100R		TR5	BUK555-60A
R13	100R		TR6	BUK555-60A
R14	100R		TR7	BUK555-60A
Rv1	1K0, preset Maplin stock no: WR40T		TR8	BUK555-60A
Rv2	47K, preset Maplin stock no: WR43W		TR9	BUK555-60A
			IC1	ZN409CE, Electromail stock no: 304-813

Miscellaneous components

- PCB
- Terminal pins
- Wire etc

■ 10
Flasher Unit

In scale models a touch of realism can be added to the model with the inclusion of anti-collision lights. The unit described here, for example, is designed to supply the model's anti-collision lights to flash at a rate of approximately once every second. Additionally the unit can be controlled with the inclusion of the low current switch described in Chapter 5. The flasher unit can be switched on or off from the transmitter if a channel is so assigned. Otherwise the flasher unit can be run continuously in the model with the basic configuration shown in Figure 10.3. The unit is designed to run from a battery source, from six to twelve volts maximum.

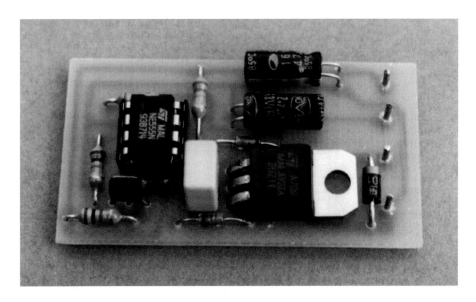

Flasher unit.

The circuit

The circuit owes nothing to originality, and is a common circuit using an LM555 timer in the familiar role as an astable multivibrator with an additional FET driver to increase the current handling capacity from 200 mA (for the 555 timer alone) to 5 A for the whole circuit.

The timing component values were chosen to give a flash rate of approximately one flash every one and a half seconds, with a short on duration of about 300 ms.

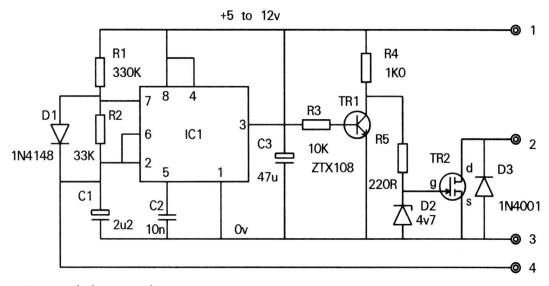

Fig. 10.1 Flasher circuit diagram.

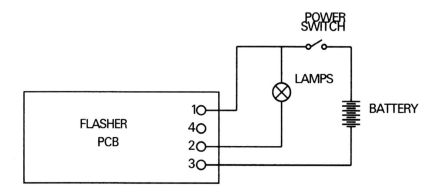

Fig. 10.2 Connection of circuit to battery and lamp.

Construction

The components are all mounted on the top side of the PCB. The timer chip is soldered into the board. The timing capacitor C1 and the supply decoupling capacitor C3 are both mounted flat to the board, so as to reduce height. A small amount of glue is used to attach the capacitor to the board to aid the survival of the component in the event of a crash.

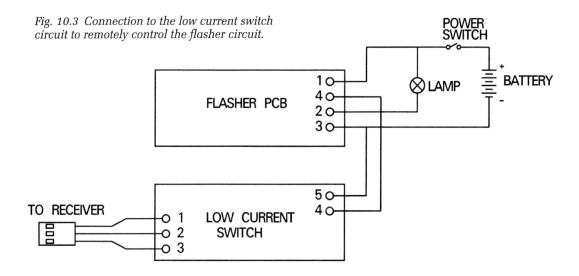

Fig. 10.3 Connection to the low current switch circuit to remotely control the flasher circuit.

Testing

Connect the completed unit as shown in Figure 10.2. Quite simply the unit should operate and the bulb should flash at approximately once every second and a half. If you wish to flash the bulb at a slower rate the timing capacitor C1 can be changed for one which is higher in value, perhaps 4.7μF which would give a flashing rate of around three seconds.

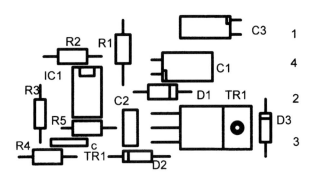

Fig. 10.4 Component layout.

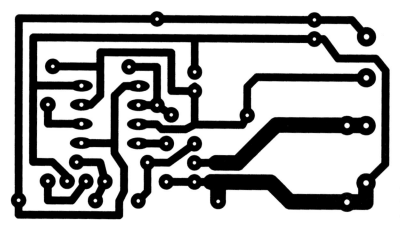

Fig. 10.5 PCB track layout shown through from component side (twice actual size).

To check the remote switching facility of the unit simply connect pin 4 on the PCB to the negative side of the battery. This will inhibit the timing capacitor from charging and the bulb will be unlit. Remove the jumper lead from pin 4, and the timing circuit will then operate and the bulb will commence flashing.

Remote operation

To add the remote operation to the model, the low current switch circuit detailed in Chapter 5 has to be constructed and set up accordingly. This has to be connected to the flasher unit as detailed in Figure 10.3. Actuating the switch on the transmitter will simply make the flasher unit switch on or off.

Component list

R1	330K all resistors are ¼ W	C2	10n
R2	33K	C3	47µF 16V radial electrolytic
R3	10K	D1	1N4148
R4	1K0	D2	4v7 400mW zener diode
R5	220R	D3	1N4148
C1	2.2µF 16V PCB mounting electrolytic	TR1	ZTX108
		TR2	BUZ11

Miscellaneous components

■ PCB
■ Terminal pins
■ Wire etc.

■ 11
Servo Splitter

The use of this small device serves to split the servo signal from one servo output and divide the signal to feed two servos mounted in the model.

Completed servo splitter.

The circuit provides isolation between the two servos, and decouples the servos from the receiver circuit.

The circuit

The circuit incorporates two transistors which are configured as what is known as an emitter-follower. Essentially the emitter-follower is a circuit often used to provide current

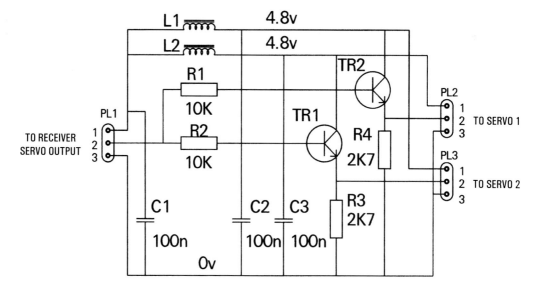

Fig. 11.1 Servo splitter.

gain, but with no actual voltage gain (no amplification). The circuit does basically what it is called, the emitter terminal voltage of the transistor *follows* the base terminal voltage. But there is a small loss of just over half a volt so the emitter voltage will be only 0.6 of a volt less than the voltage at the base terminal. The servos can cope with this insignificant voltage drop during the course of their operation without any adverse affects.

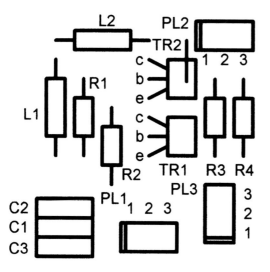

Fig. 11.2 Component layout.

Chokes L1 and L2 are added to the circuit which offer some degree of isolation on the power supply lines. This helps in reducing the effect of interference between motors in the model, albeit servo to servo or motive motor to servo. The addition of the power supply decoupling capacitors serves as a pi-filter and further reduces the problem of electrical noise.

Construction

The components are mounted close to the board. Three pin PCB mounting plugs are mounted on the PCB and serve to provide power and signals from the receiver and to the servos being used. Cable-mounted sockets then make the connections to the receiver and the servos.

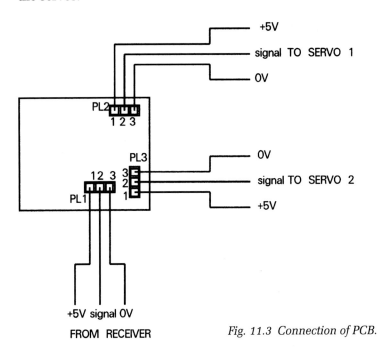

Fig. 11.3 Connection of PCB.

Checking the unit

No setting up is required as there are few components to consider. However, it is possible to check the operation of the circuit.

Connect the unit to a five volt supply – a 4.8 V receiver nicad pack will suffice. Ensure that the power to the board is as follows, positive to pin 1 of PL1 and negative to pin 3 of pin 3. With the aid of a multimeter, measure the voltage at these points, ensure the negative probe of the multimeter is attached to the negative side of the 5 V supply.

PL2 pin 1   5V

PL3 pin 1   5V

Connect pin 2 of PL1 to the negative supply of the 5 V source, check the voltage at the following points;

PL2 pin 2   0V

PL3 pin 2   0V

Connect pin 2 of PL1 to the positive supply of the 5 V source (i.e. 5.0 V), check the voltage at the following points;

PL2 pin 2   4.4V (approx.)

PL3 pin 2   4.4V (approx.)

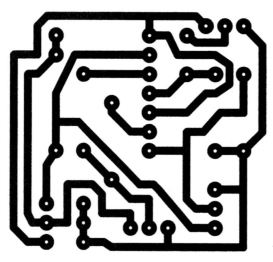

Fig. 11.4 PCB track layout shown through from component side (twice actual size).

Components list

R1   10K

R2   10K

R3   2K7

R4   2K7

C1   100nF

C2   100nF

C3   100nF

TR1 ZTX108

TR2 ZTX108

L1   100uH choke

L2   100uH choke

Miscellaneous components

■ PL1,2 and 3 PCB mounting 3-way plugs
■ PCB

Appendix A
List of Component Suppliers

Electronic component suppliers

Maplin Electronics
PO Box 3
Rayleigh
Essex
SS6 8LR
UK

Farnell Electronic Components
Canal Road
Leeds
LS12 2TU
UK

Manufacturer of printed circuit boards

P & D Circuits
Unit 2
Power Works
Slade Green Road
Erith
Kent
DA8 2HU
UK

RS components retail outlets

Electromail
PO Box 33
Corby
Northants
NN17 9EL
UK

Greenweld Electronic Components
27 Park Road
Southampton
Hants
SO15 3UQ
UK

Appendix B
Pin Component Designation

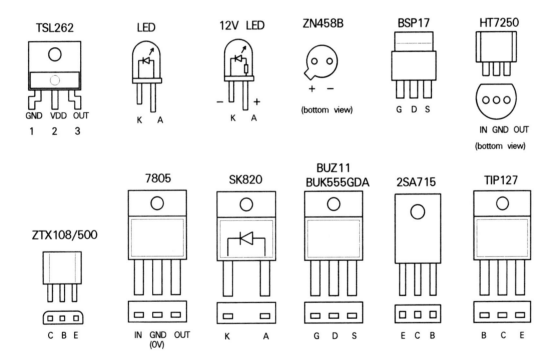

TSL262
GND VDD OUT
1   2   3

LED
K   A

12V LED
−   +
K   A

ZN458B
+   −
(bottom view)

BSP17
G   D   S

HT7250
IN GND OUT
(bottom view)

ZTX108/500
C B E

7805
IN GND OUT
(0V)

SK820
K   A

BUZ11
BUK555GDA
G   D   S

2SA715
E C B

TIP127
B C E